KHIROKITIA

SERIES OF GUIDE BOOKS

KHIROKITIA
A NEOLITHIC SITE

Text by
Alain Le Brun

ΠΟΛΙΤΙΣΤΙΚΟ ΙΔΡΥΜΑ
ΤΡΑΠΕΖΗΣ ΚΥΠΡΟΥ

BANK OF CYPRUS CULTURAL FOUNDATION
IN COLLABORATION WITH THE DEPARTMENT OF ANTIQUITIES

NICOSIA 1997

ISBN 9963-42-061-3

CONTENTS

In memory of Evangelos L. Louizos

In 1987 the Bank of Cyprus Cultural Foundation instigated a programme of publication of archaeological guides for Cyprus. The money raised by the sale of the guides is offered to the Department of Antiquities for the conservation and restoration of ancient monuments.

The Cultural Foundation has already published the Guide to Kourion, the Guide to the Mosaics of Paphos and the Guide to the House of the Dragoman of Cyprus, Hadjigeorgakis Kornessios in four languages: Greek, English, French and German. The present guide is concerned with the neolithic settlement of Khirokitia. The text was written by Monsieur Alain Le Brun, Director of the French Archaeological Mission to Khirokitia since 1976. The text on the archaeological park, published as an appendix, is by Mr S. Hadjisavvas, Curator of Monuments in the Department of Antiquities of Cyprus.

The Cultural Foundation would like to thank all those who contributed to this edition, in particular Mrs Louise Steel for the English translation, Mrs O. Daune-Le Brun for the drawings (figs 1, 5, 8, 12, 18, 21, 48), and Mr Y. Hadjisavvas, in charge of the photographic archive of the Cyprus Museum. The colour photographs were taken by the French Archaeological Mission to Khirokitia, with the exception of fig. 4, from the French Mission at Amathus, and figs 22, 25-26, 32, which were taken by Mr A. Metaxas with the permission of the Department of Antiquities. Figs 2, 20, 14-47 are from the excavations of P. Dikaios and were reproduced with kind permission of the Department of Antiquities. Costoula Sclavenitis was responsible for the revision of the English text. The edition of this guide was prepared by Marie-Lise Mitsou.

Andreas Patsalides
President of the Bank of Cyprus
Cultural Foundation

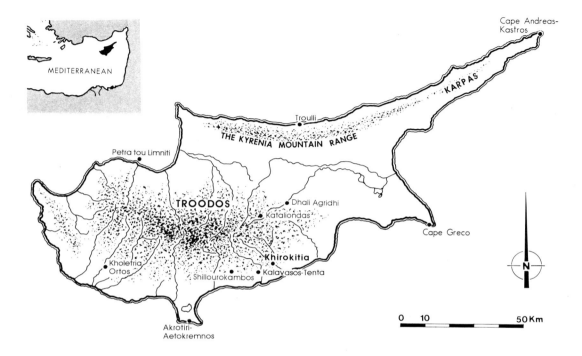

Fig. 1. The main aceramic neolithic sites of Cyprus

Fig. 2. Excavation of zone A, 1937 campaign (pp. 8-9)

SINCE THE MIOCENE the island of Cyprus has been cut off from the mainland – a continent where man appeared very early and where, between the tenth and the eighth millennia, it is possible to follow the progression from hunter-gatherer societies to the first agropastoral civilizations, to see the foundation of the first villages, to witness the domestication of plants and animals and to see man acquire new technical skills. This progressive transformation, or neolithization, is not apparent on Cyprus. During the tenth millennium BC man made an unobtrusive and brief appearance on the island, as is witnessed at the site of Akrotiri-Aetokremnos, but this is followed by a long period for which nothing is known. Then suddenly, around 7000 BC (a calibrated date, that is to say a carbon-14 date corrected by correlations with dendrochronology), or perhaps a little earlier, we see village communities prospering on the island. The inhabitants practised agriculture and animal husbandry, exploiting domesticated species of plants and animals whose wild ancestors were unknown on the island.

This civilization, the aceramic Neolithic – so-called because ceramic technology was unknown on the island– is represented by Khirokitia, and by twenty or so other settlements scattered throughout the island: from Cape Andreas-Kastros in the extreme east to Kholetria-Ortos in the west, from Troulli and Petra tou Limniti in the north, to Kalavasos-Tenta and Shillourokambos, as well as Khirokitia, in the south, and not forgetting the inland sites of Dhali-Agridhi and Kataliondas, to mention only those sites which have been explored archaeologically (fig. 1).

History of Research

The site of Khirokitia was discovered in 1934 by P. Dikaios, who conducted six campaigns there between 1936 and 1946, under the auspices of the Department of Antiquities (fig. 2). As well as the remains of numerous houses cleared in zones A, B and C, the excavations also revealed the traces of a linear stone structure for almost 185 m, preserved in places to a height of 3.5 m and crossing right through the site from north to south. The discovery of architectural remains on such a scale, together with the absence of pottery, dramatically confirmed the existence of an aceramic episode on the island, as had already been hinted in 1929 by excavations on the small island of Petra tou Limniti by the Swedish Cyprus Expedition.

The exploration of the site was only resumed in the 1970s. In 1972 the Department of Antiquities of the Republic of Cyprus carried out two brief operations: a trial trench, which today is filled in, was sunk in the north of zone C, and unit XII was partially excavated in zone A.

The invasion of the island in 1974 by the Turkish army forced the Cypriot authorities to reorientate archaeological activity. They therefore decided to reopen Khirokitia as part of a new research program. An exploratory campaign in 1976 identified the limits of the site and determined where best to sink a new trench. This was opened the following year, on the summit of the hill in zone D (fig. 3), by a French mission sponsored by the CNRS (the National Scientific Research Centre) and the General Department of Cultural, Scientific and Technical Relations of the French Ministry of Foreign Affairs.

Climate and Environment

Today Cyprus enjoys a Mediterranean climate, with a strong contrast between seasons: hot dry summers from July to September, mild, rainy winters from November to March, separated by brief, changeable springs and autumns covering the months of April-May and October respectively. The mean annual precipitation recorded for the south of the island is 400 to 500 mm, and is spread over November/December to March.

Pollen analysis reveals an almost identical picture during the neolithic period. The rare arboreal species present from the most ancient levels –that is to say from the time that the site was occupied by man– are thermophile, or basically Mediterranean. Their presence and their sporadic, yet regular persistence suggest a constant, warm, dry climate. The various pollen samples likewise reveal a sparsely wooded landscape, similar to that of today, contrary to anthracological analyses.

A Closed Village

Situated in the Maroni valley, about 6 km as the crow flies from the sea, the site of Khirokitia lies in a relatively uneven landscape, in the foothills of the Troodhos massif. The remains of the neolithic village, or more precisely of the successive villages, as the site was occupied continuously throughout the aceramic neolithic period, spread over the sides of a hill. It is enclosed to the north, east, and southeast by a deep bend in the Maroni river, and to the west it adjoins the neighbouring high hills (figs 4 and 5). The built-up area is crossed from north to south by a linear stone structure (fig. 5: structure 100, fig. 6) dividing the settlement into two sectors: the east and west sectors. P. Dikaios, who discovered this structure, interpreted it as the main road, or backbone, of the settlement. According to Dikaios, on the one hand the east and west sectors were occupied simultaneously and on the other hand this structure was situated in the centre of the village, meeting the inhabitants' supposed need for a thoroughfare. The village, therefore, was articulated along a "main road".

The resumption of excavations has revealed quite a different picture. Actually, it appears that the growth of the site towards the west was far more limited than would appear from the configuration

Fig. 3. General view of zone D

13

of the hill in that area, which is apparently quite suitable for occupation. It is also evident that the extent of the site in the east was considerable. So rather than being central, the position of the road was in fact peripheral. Moreover, excavations on the summit of the hill, in zone D, far from confirming the presumed contemporaneity of the east and west sectors, have instead shown that the east sector was occupied *before* the west sector, and that the "road" was built *before* the occupation of the west sector.

These findings called for another interpretation of the emplacement of the settlement, more in keeping with its topography – a quick glance at the general plan (fig. 5) is sufficient to confirm it: that of a village that was separated from the outside world from the moment of its foundation by a wall which blocked the hill, thus completing its natural protection as offered by a bend in the river (fig. 7) and the partial escarpment of the hill where it is absent. This wall, a massive pisé structure, its exterior facade revetted in stone, was

Fig. 4. Aerial view of the site of Khirokitia

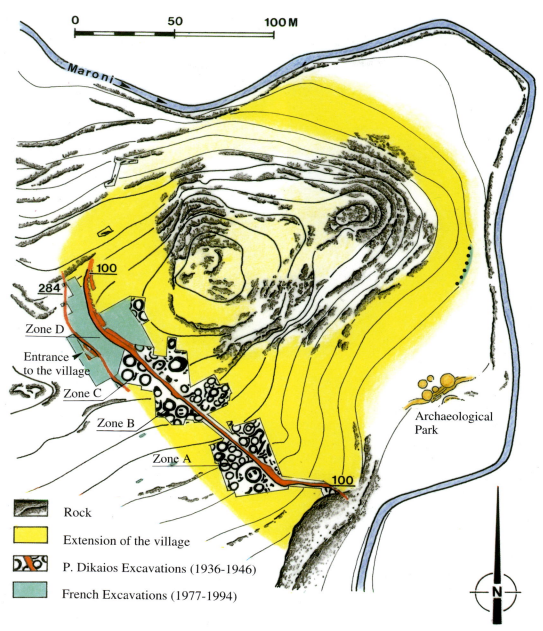

0   50   100 M

Maroni

100

284

Zone D

Entrance
to the village

Zone C

Zone B

Zone A

100

Archaeological
Park

Rock

Extension of the village

P. Dikaios Excavations (1936-1946)

French Excavations (1977-1994)

N

Fig. 5. General plan of the site of Khirokitia

15

Fig. 6. Exterior face of the first enclosure wall,
with a later structure to the left

Fig. 7. The bed of the Maroni river at the foot
of the site

modified on several ococcasions without, however, significantly altering its course. The wall remained in use until the village spread beyond its boundaries towards the west, onto land which up till then had remained unoccupied. The reasons for this are not as yet clear, but it was perhaps due to an increase in population.

The same pattern was again repeated. The new land was in turn enclosed by an impressive stone wall, 2.5 m thick, preserved to a maximum height of more than 3 m, the line of which has been traced for more than 60 m (fig. 5: structure 284).

Therefore, rather than an open village articulated along a central road, Khirokitia was in fact an enclosed village: enclosed naturally by the escarpment and artificially by the wall. The construction of the wall is an important example of collective effort, with few known parallels in the Near East. This is suggestive of a social organization which was sufficiently structured to orchestrate the necessary labour to construct and maintain works of this scale for the common good.

The defensive nature of these works appears self-evident. Various surveys conducted on Cyprus, however, have shown that the island was then sparsely populated, and it is difficult to envisage territorial rivalry to such a degree that it would have been necessary to build defensive structures of this size. It is true that the desire for new land is not the only cause of violence. Yet, unless we assume that weapons were made solely from perishable materials, then, as far as we can tell from recovered material, military equipment is particularly poorly represented, if not non-existent. Moreover, no traces of hostilities, such as fires, destruction levels, or examples of violent death, have yet been uncovered. Whatever they were, these walls represent the limit separating the built-up zone from the zone with no buildings, the inhabited territory from the outside world, and are indicative of the high price that was attached to the inhabited land.

Access to the Village

Although the village was thought of as an enclosed world, and treated as such, it communicated with the outside world by one, or more probably, given its extent, by several access points. Two of these, used at different stages during the occupation of the site, have been identified in zone D. Little survives of the older access point, which was partially destroyed and obliterated by later structures. On the other hand, the more recent one, which

has been reconstructed identically at the foot of the site, is in an excellent state of preservation (figs 8 and 49). Rather than a simple opening in the village enclosure wall, it is in fact a complex architectural system, designed to overcome the difference in height of more than 2 m between the surface on which the village was built and the lower ground outside, as well as to control access to the village.

This complex, unique to Cyprus and the Near East, shows the full extent of the exceptional technical skill of the inhabitants of Khirokitia. It comprises a stairway integrated within a large, quadrangular, stone structure, more than 10 m long and 1.6 m deep, which lies against the exterior face of the village enclosure wall.

The stairway, with steps 0.8 m wide, 0.3 to 0.4 m high and 0.45 m deep, comprises three flights at right angles to each other. The middle flight, nestled in the core of the structure, is hidden from view.

The entrance to the village is controlled by the narrowness of the stairway, by its tortuous route, and also by an imposing structure, preserved to a height of almost 2.5 m, which rises to almost 2 m in front of the opening of the stairway and prevents direct access. Whether it was an isolated structure, a kind of prominent bastion which had to be by-passed, or else another wall which in its turn required an entrance should be clarified by

Fig. 8.   Reconstruction of one of the entrances to the village

investigations that are currently underway. Whatever the case, the size of the structure, the enormous investment in time and labour that it represents, and the series of obstacles ensuring the strict control of access to the village are indicative of the wish to live inside an enclosed world. Let us now consider the architectural units within this enclosed world. How were they organized? But first what were they and how were they built?

Building Techniques

The basic architectural unit is a structure with a circular ground plan, the exterior diameter of which varies between 2.3 and 9.2 m and the interior diameter between 1.4 and 4.8 m (fig. 3). Before construction begins the surface is more or less carefully prepared: it is roughly levelled and sometimes given a coating. The walls are built directly onto the underlying deposits, with no foundation trench (fig. 9).

The materials used are stone –blocks of light-coloured limestone collected on the surface and dark diabase pebbles from the river-bed– pisé and mudbrick, made from earth mixed with straw and dried in the sun. These materials are used either singly or in combination with each other. Thus we find walls made of stones set on one or two courses and bonded with mud mortar; mudbrick or pisé walls; walls made of stones embedded in pisé; or even walls built in two concentric rings, the outer one of stones, and the inner one of

pisé or mudbricks, these latter sometimes resting on a stone substructure. The internal and external faces of the wall are covered by a whitish earth plaster. Sometimes flat stones, set on edge around the base of the wall, protect it from erosion by rain water.

The unit is entered through an opening in the wall, usually around 0.5 m wide, and frequently with a paved threshold (figs 14 and 50). The doorway, which might not be on the same level with the floor, is reached by one or more steps. Usually the wall has no other entrance, though some might have small openings to let air and light into the building. The most notable example is a unit in zone D, which has no less than three windows, with an average width of 0.45 m, at regular intervals (figs 10 and 50).

The roof is flat and not domed, as the apparent inward curvature of the walls, caused by the pressure of the earth, and the absence of post-holes or of any traces of support, might suggest. This was proven by the discovery of numerous fragments of burnt earth –the collapsed remains of the roof– strewn over the floor in a unit which had accidentally been destroyed by fire (fig. 11). These fragments, some of which are on display in the Larnaca Museum, are flat. Moreover, on one side there are the impressions of plants of varying sizes, that have enabled us to establish the different materials used in the roofing and how they were put together (fig. 12). First, there is a wooden frame resting on the top of the unit's wall. This frame supported two crossed layers of plants, probably reeds, covered by several layers of pisé and earth. The floors were covered by an earth plaster of varying quality, and were periodically replastered straight onto the underlying deposits, or less frequently onto a layer of small stones, large pebbles, or even mudbricks. The plaster continued over the interior face of the wall and could also serve as a base for painted mural decora-tion, as could the plaster that covered the surface of the piers inside some units (fig. 13). Due to the bad state of preservation of the painted decoration discovered at Khirokitia, it is not possible to say wheth-er it comprised geometric motifs or fig-ured decoration, like the example found at the neighbouring site of Kalavasos-Tenta, a fragment of which is on display in the Cyprus Museum, Nicosia. The fact that wall-painting is so well attested at both these sites goes some way towards

Fig. 9.   Section of a stone unit on the remains of a mudbrick unit

Fig. 10.   A window (zone D, unit S. 125)

Fig. 11.   Fragment of roof

placing the Cypriot aceramic Neolithic within a cultural tradition whose beginnings can be traced back to the ninth millennium BC in the Near East.

The House and the Village

The floor comprised different installations according to the use or uses to which each unit was put (figs 14, 15 and 51). Some –steps, low walls and platforms, usually trapezoidal– were used to divide the space and define work and rest areas, while others –bowls, basins and hearths– were installations of a domestic character. Partitioned and cluttered by such equipment, it appears that the usable surface in some cases, such as in figure 15 or as in unit IA (fig. 41), one of the first units which the visitor to the site will see, might be increased by a platform resting on large stone piers, which alone have survived.

Each of these units, with their diverse internal arrangements, is part of a larger

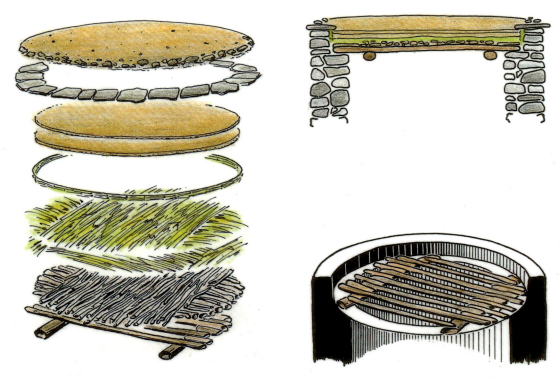

Fig. 12.   *Reconstruction of the roof of a dwelling unit*

domestic space: the house. Its ideal form, as can be reconstructed from the excavations at Khirokitia, may be defined as a compound of several of these circular units around an unroofed space, a sort of small inner "courtyard". Inside the courtyard there was an installation for grinding grain: a fixed quern surrounded by pebble paving (fig. 16). The total domestic space thus constituted, large enough to shelter a family, is the place of various spatially defined daily activities: grain was ground within the limits of the house, but outside the units, in the courtyard; whereas cooking took place inside the units, on a special type of hearth that is only found inside covered areas. These hearths (fig. 17), which were designed only to hold charcoal from fires lit outside the unit, are placed on a small rectangular platform covered by a stone slab or a paving of small pebbles, which act as refractive plates, thus keeping smoke to a minimum.

Figure 18 shows one of these houses in zone D. There are seven circular units of

Fig. 13.   Wall-painting (zone D, unit S. 122)

Fig. 14.   Unit (zone D, S. 94)

Fig. 15.   Unit (zone D, S. 122)

varying size, with doorways 0.5 m wide opening onto an uncovered space which is equipped with a grinding installation. The small unit in the foreground might have been a storage area. No equipment was found on its floor, which was placed on a foundation of small pebbles. Not all the units need have served the same function within the economy of the house. Some were equipped with a hearth while others were not. Moreover, a study of the spatial organization of material found inside the units –such as sets of flint tools, stone vessels, and bone tools– leads to the same conclusion and also allows us to identify zones of specialized activity inside some of the units.

The houses thus identified are crowded one against the other, only separated by narrow strips of land, which were used as passageways and for the disposal of rubbish. The dense fabric of the village's built-up area is interrupted here and there by empty spaces without any domestic equipment or any other trace of activity, domestic or otherwise, and yet the surface

Fig. 16.   Installation for grinding grain (zone D)

Fig. 17.   A hearth (zone D, unit S. 125)

Fig. 18. A house, reconstruction

of these areas is carefully plastered. They should not, therefore, be treated as waste or abandoned ground; instead, empty though these spaces appear to us, their inclusion into the built-up area seems to suggest that they were reserved for uses associated with other aspects of the life and concerns of the community.

The village stretches in a vast semicircle around the steepest and highest part of the hill (fig. 5), covering an area which can be estimated at *c.* 1.5 ha. This estimate includes the full extent of the village during all phases of occupation, ignoring fluctuations in the area of occupation – which, as we saw earlier, was first established in the east and later extended towards the west. Also, this estimation, together with information concerning the density of occupation recovered during the excavations in zone D, can only give a maximum approximation as to the size of the population. Taking these reservations into consideration and assuming that the total area of the settlement was occupied concurrently in time, and in a continuous and uniform way spatially, the maximum population at Khirokitia lies between 300 and 600 inhabitants, but was no doubt closer to 300 than 600.

The People

Of small stature —on average the men were 1.61 m and the women 1.51 m— the inhabitants of Khirokitia were brachyce-phalic (short-skulled), a feature which in many cases was accentuated by artificial flattening of the occipital part of the skull. It appears that this practice was more frequent on women than on men, and was achieved by fixing a board, held in place by bandages, which compressed the back of the skull. The infant mortality rate was high and life expectancy was 22 years. The average age reached by adults was around 35 years for men and 33 years for women.

Man and his Beliefs

No cult place has been found at Khirokitia nor at any of the other excavated aceramic sites. Funerary practices, wall paintings, and figurines are the only documents, often of an ambiguous and fragmentary nature, likely to throw light upon the mental world and the deeper preoccupations of the people of neolithic Cyprus.

As well as the living, the habitation area also belonged to the dead. Indeed the dead were buried in pits inside the units

(fig. 19) which, however, were not abandoned. After the body was placed in the pit it was filled with earth and covered with a layer of plaster, which subsequently served as the floor of the dwelling. The dead therefore remained with the living, and death did not separate a human community that was characterized by its wish to live within an enclosed space. The burials were single, primary inhumations, that is to say the body was placed in the ground before decomposition caused the skeleton to become disarticulated. The body was usually laid out on its right side, although it might be laid out on its left side, on its back, or more rarely on the stomach. It might equally be laid out partly on one side and partly on the stomach or back. The body was placed in a contracted position and it appears that the degree of contraction varied according to the age of the deceased. Most adults were laid out in a hypercontracted position. The orientation of the skull was variable, although it was not totally haphazard, and reveals discrete sexual differentiation.

The provision of grave gifts —both everyday objects and objects more specifically related to funerary ritual— is not the general rule (fig. 20) and is more frequent with female than male burials. Even so, the sex of the deceased appears to have determined the type of object placed in the grave. Necklaces of alternating shell (dentalium) and stone (cornelian) beads are only found with female burials (fig. 43), and stone vases, often intentionally broken or put out of use, more frequently

Fig. 19. Three burials inside a unit (zone D, unit S. 97)

accompanied females than males. On the other hand, a heavy stone, carved or unworked, placed on the body –as though to prevent the dead from returning to the world of the living– is twice as common in male than in female burials (fig. 19).

The complexity of funerary ritual is well illustrated by a burial whose excavation has enabled us to reconstruct the series of "ritual acts", or some of these acts, which accompanied the inhumation of an adult female (fig. 21). Once the pit was dug

inside the unit, two stone vessels were deposited in it: a small stone bowl broken into three pieces and a large basin placed upside down, whose base was smashed *in situ*. Next the body was placed in the pit, its head resting on the large stone basin. The body was then covered by a large worked stone, on which a third stone bowl, also broken into many pieces, was placed. Finally, the pit was filled in and sealed by a layer of mud.

Wall-paintings found *in situ* are very rare

Fig. 20.   A burial (zone A, Miscellaneous Grave IX), 1938 campaign

and are too badly preserved to be understood, or even read. The clearest specimen, which comes from Kalavasos-Tenta and has the remains of a composition depicting two human figures, one of which has raised arms –also the attitude of a figure decorating a stone bowl from Khirokitia and evocative of some figures from the Anatolian site of Catal Hüyük– allows us only to conclude that representation of the human figure formed part of the iconographic repertoire.

The human figure is also the primary subject of figurines: representations of animals are rare and do not include any species exploited by man. In this respect the Cypriot aceramic neolithic phase is no different from the civilizations of the Near East.

With the exception of a head modelled in clay (fig. 22), now in the Cyprus Museum, Nicosia, all the figurines found at Khirokitia are made of stone. Some figures are simple silhouettes carved on a small pebble by lateral nicks, sometimes completed by a vertical stroke indicating

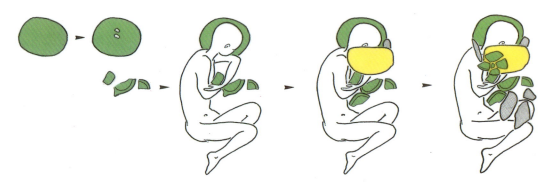

Fig. 21.   Reconstruction of one of the funerary rituals seen at Khirokitia

Fig. 22.   Head modelled in clay

Fig. 23.   Anthropomorphic figurine, diabase

the legs (fig. 23); others are more abstract, with the body as an elongated appendage surmounted by a disc-shaped head (fig. 24). There are also more elaborate carved pieces where simple geometric bulk gives the body volume (fig. 25). Finally, there are larger figurines, only the heads of which survive, often with detailed representations of various features (fig. 26).

These figurines, which are of various shapes and sizes, probably served different purposes, but the contexts in which they are found do not allow greater precision. The absence of any indication of sex is particularly striking. Even if some of the figurines do have an unmistakable phallic appearance, it is always allusive. This circumspect representation of the male sex, and above all the absence of women in the imagery of the aceramic Neolithic on Cyprus, is even more remarkable considering that from the ninth millennium BC onwards representations of the human form, especially those of females, abound in the Near East.

Tools

Chert, flint, limestone, diabase, and animal bones (frequently the metatarsals of fallow deer) are the principal materials used by the inhabitants of Khirokitia to manufacture tools. Although known and used in architecture, the plastic properties of clay were not exploited for the manufacture of vessels: rare experiments were made using clay, but these were not followed up.

Chipped stone tools, of flint and chert (fig. 27), comprise various pieces, principally natural backed flakes which appear to have been highly prized, or short unretouched blades. Some of the blades were retouched, along the back, in part or completely, either in a straight or a convex line, and may show a gloss on their cutting edge. Microscopic trace-wear analysis of these tools indicates that they were used in a range of activities – both in foraging and manufacturing– for a

Fig. 24. Anthropomorphic figurine, diabase

31

Fig. 25. *Anthropomorphic figurine, diabase*   Fig. 26.   *Anthropomorphic figurine, diabase*

variety of tasks, such as harvesting cereals, and also cutting reeds (used for roofing and bedding), wood-working (to strip bark and saw), and scraping fresh skins.

The toolkit also includes notched and denticulated pieces, and a small number of burins, some flake or blade scrapers, and rare perforating tools. Paradoxically, although hunting is well attested, arrowheads are lacking. This absence of arrowheads, and also of the retouching technique (retouched by flat pressure), the

monotony and the rudimentary character of this industry, all distinguish it from contemporary industries in neighbouring areas.

Bone tools are relatively abundant, but with little variety, and in the main comprise tools associated with manufacture: pointed tools, principally tools for perforation (fig. 28), some of which were fixed in handles made of deer antlers, fine needles with eyes (fig. 29) used for sewing, or larger pierced tools, intended to join fibres or threads; that is to say tools used in basketry, to make nets, or to weave material, for which we know they had the technical know-how (fig. 30). On the other hand, tools associated with working skins, such as smoothing tools, are absent.

Stone was used to make cutting implements, grinding, pounding and crushing stones, and containers, as well as for jewellery.

The cutting implements are axes made by pecking and polishing diabase pebbles.

Grinding, pounding and crushing implements comprise flat or saddle querns, handstones, pounders, grinders, and occasional pestles. Flat pebbles with traces of red pigment may have been used as palettes.

Receptacles made from perishable materials –wood, basketwork, skins– were no doubt used, but nothing survives of these. Stone vessels, on the other hand, are numerous, of varying forms, and can be divided into two large categories: coarse

Fig. 27.   Chipped stone tools

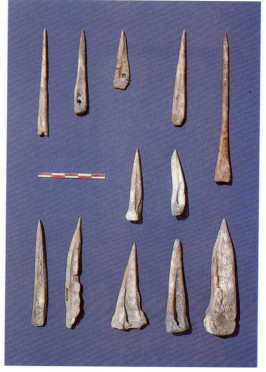

Fig. 28.   Bone tool

vessels and fine vessels. The coarse vessels comprise trays and basins hollowed out from slabs or blocks of breccia or hard limestone. The finer vessels include bowls and basins made by scraping fragments of soft limestone, and receptacles made from hard stone, diabase, which are particularly characteristic of the Cypriot aceramic Neolithic (fig. 31). From several roughed out pieces abandoned at different stages of manufacture we can reconstruct how they were made. First a circular channel was cut around the central part of the surface of the pebble which was to be hollowed out, and this was then removed by shattering. A new channel was then cut and the process was repeated until the desired depth was reached. The vessel was finished by being pecked out and polished. The vessel forms include trays, cups, bowls, basins, and spoons. The bowls and basins might have a spout, a horizontal or vertical handle, or just a tenon. Such attachments, as well as the decorations which adorn some of the vessels, are indicative of great skill in work-

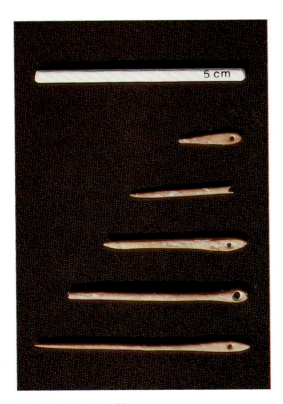

Fig. 29.   Needle with eye

Fig. 30.   Fragment of mineralized material

ing stone. With the exception of a representation of a human figure on a bowl, mentioned above, the motifs are geometric. They include vertical or oblique lines, and incised chevrons, but more usually they are cut in relief and take the form of ribs – straight or curved, single or double, vertical, oblique, or arranged in zigzags. The basin reproduced in figure 32, which is on display in the Cyprus Museum, Nicosia, is a good example of the exceptional technical skill and the high aesthetic sense of these artisans.

Rocks of various origins were used to make articles of jewellery, pendants and beads (fig. 33), such as cornelian, which is not native to Cyprus, or picrolite, which is found in abundance on the Kouris river bed, west of Limassol, in the form of small rounded pebbles. Picrolite must have been brought to Khirokitia in an unworked state –like some twenty or so uncut pebbles found concealed in a unit– where it was then worked. There must have been some form of supply network in operation, as is indicated by

Fig. 31. Diabase vessels

the occurrence of picrolite objects amongst the material recovered from the small fishing village of Cape Andreas-Kastros, in the extreme east of Cyprus.

Picrolite is also one of the stones used to make "dress pins" of uncertain function. These are open rings with a pointed protrusion, in the form of a question mark, or with two points, rather like two opposed question marks. Also enigmatic are the incised basalt pebbles, which have only been found at Khirokitia and Kole-tria-Ortos, in the west of the island. These are flat pebbles (fig. 34) with a grid of incised lines on one or both of the two faces, or conical stones (fig. 35), sometimes constricted by a horizontal groove, the base of which is decorated with a quadrille pattern, while the sides are incised with a chevron motif.

The Economy

Agriculture (fig. 36), animal husbandry, and hunting provided the necessary food

Fig. 32.   Diabase basin

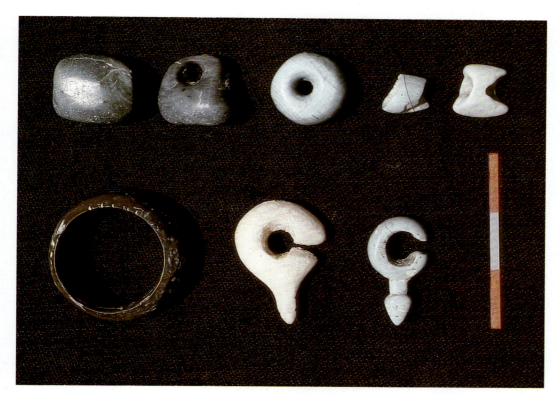

Fig. 33.   Stone jewellery

resources. As Khirokitia was some distance from the coast, seafood played a limited role in the village's economy, and fish bones recovered from the site are not numerous. The fish species represented include grouper, chrysophrys, sar, sea perch, and mullet. The fish were carefully selected for size –small fish are not represented among the remains recovered– and were brought to the site, probably fresh and whole, to be eaten. The size of the fish caught indicates elaborate fishing techniques, and that fine-meshed nets or lines armed with sturdy fish hooks must have been used.

Analysis of numerous carbonized grains retrieved through flotation of sediments reveals that agriculture was cereal based; wheat (fig. 37): einkorn wheat *(Triticum monococcum)*, emmer wheat *(T. dicoccum)*, as well as smaller quantities of barley *(Hordeum sp.)* (fig. 38) were cultivated. There is, moreover, cultivable land close to the neolithic village, notably to the west and the south: this represents 60% of a territory covered by 45 minutes

Figs 34-35. Engraved pebbles

walk (fig. 39). P. Dikaios pointed out that when the site was discovered the slopes of the hill themselves were cultivated. The grain was harvested with sickles made from small blades of flint and chert, which can be identified by the gloss on their cutting edge due to the silica contained in the stalks of the grasses. These small blades were fixed in a handle made of a perishable material, wood or bone, with a natural glue, traces of which are still sometimes visible. The grain was ground on querns, usually installed inside the courtyard of the houses. Besides cereals, legumes, such as lentils *(Lens culinaris)*, were also cultivated.

In addition to these cultivated products, fruit was collected from wild trees: pistachios, figs, olives, and plums.

The four species of large mammal identified at Khirokitia –fallow deer, sheep, goats, and pigs– which constitute more than 95% of the faunal assemblage, were exploited by man.

The fallow deer was hunted using tech-

Fig. 36.   The countryside around the site, in spring

Fig. 37.   Carbonized wheat grain

Fig. 38.   Imprint of barley on an unfired mudbrick

niques which remain unknown. The absence of arrowheads among the lithic assemblage implies the use of less elaborate weapons: handled flint blades, or wooden spears with fire-hardened points, or traps.

Sheep, goats and pigs were reared and kept outside the village. No trace of an enclosure capable of holding animals has been located within the village perimeter, and moreover the narrow entrance would not lend itself to the movement of animals.

The methods used to rear animals appear to have improved during the occupation of the site and were increasingly better controlled, as indicated by the gradual increase in the percentage of ovines in comparison with the percentage of both pigs and deer.

Cyprus and the Continent

Khirokitia, like the other aceramic sites on the island, was abandoned suddenly and the island appears to have remained free of human habitation for a rather long period, until the emergence of a new civilization, the ceramic Neolithic. Khirokitia was also reoccupied at this time, but no architectural traces of this reoccupation survive. With the evidence at our disposal it is impossible to make sense of this abandonment and its abruptness. Palynological studies give no indication of changes in climatic conditions which would have destroyed the ecological equilibrium of the island and brought about a dramatic decrease in food resources. No traces of a natural catastrophe or epidemic, or violent destructions caused by human agents have been found, and we are in no position to detect any possible changes in socio-economic factors.

This uncertainty marking the end of the aceramic Neolithic is also characteristic of its beginnings. Nothing has been found in Cyprus to foreshadow the sudden emergence of a civilization which appears fully formed on the island and is distinct in a number of ways from other civilizations known on the continent. There are, however, several indications of a link between Cyprus and the continent, suggesting that the island was populated by a colonization. This implies crossing a stretch of the sea, and we know that since the Upper Palaeolithic people in the east Mediterranean had mastered the art of navigation. First, we see the presence on Cypriot sites of raw material foreign to the island, such as cornelian and obsidian, which was therefore imported.

There is also the fauna, which is made up of species new to the island –fallow deer, sheep, goats, pigs, and also cats, dogs, and foxes– taking the place of the pygmy hippopotami and dwarf elephants which lived on Cyprus during the Pleistocene. No doubt deer and pigs theoretically are capable of swimming across the stretch of the sea separating Cyprus from the mainland, but this performance appears more implausible for sheep and goats, let alone cats. It is also reasonable to assume that the assemblage of cereals and legumes found on Cypriot sites were introduced to the island by man, because even if the undomesticated forms of some of these plants existed previously on Cyprus, it is the domestic forms that are found in the neolithic villages. In other words, even if it were not the plants themselves which were introduced in a domesticated form, the knowledge of the processes leading to their domestication was. Finally, the use of wall-paintings, as well as knowledge of the techniques of stone polishing and weaving, all place Cyprus within a general cultural context.

If all this evidence speaks in favour of a colonization, it is, however, insufficient to identify the point of departure of the colonists, and at best can only give an imprecise indication of their origin. For example, even supposing that the natural habitat of the *Dama mesopotamica* –and the morphological characteristics of the Cypriot fallow deer indicate it to be a subspecies of this– has not undergone significant modifications during the course of time, the import of these animals to the island points back to the Levant. Once we accept that the appearance of the aceramic Neolithic on the island occurred at the transition between the eighth and seventh millennium BC, the inclusion of Cyprus in a general context implies that the colonization of this new land should be understood in a similar way to the occupation, on the mainland, of the temperate coastal zone, or the reoccupation of the desert banks of the Euphrates, of the inland oases of Syria and Jordan, and of the Sinai – i.e. as one of a number of episodes of neolithic geographic expansion, or one of a number of episodes of a phenomenon known as "the neolithic exodus".

Fig. 39.   The hill, with the neolithic village, in spring

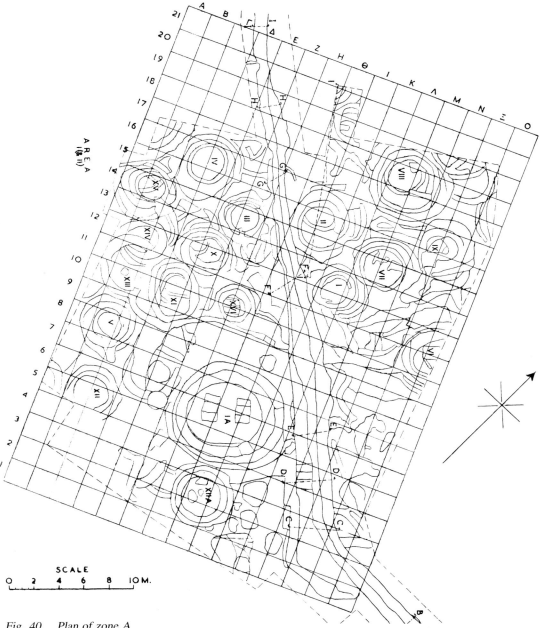

Fig. 40.   Plan of zone A

VISITING THE SITE

The first constructions that the visitor will see, once past the guards' house, are an identical replica of a portion of the village enclosure wall, and one of the entrances through the latter, such as has been found by the archaeologists during their exploration of zone D, on the summit of the hill. The information recovered during excavation has been used in the same way to work out the plans and dimensions of the units, the dimensions and nature of their openings, the form and construction of the roof, and the internal arrangement of the units. Likewise, species of trees identified by the analysis of wood carbon recovered from the site have been planted in the vicinity of this reconstruction.

From here a ramp takes the visitor up to the archaeological site. From the start visitors should be aware of the inaccuracy of the image before their eyes. The village appears to be divided into four zones, A, B, C, and D, but this division is artificial and not supported by any archaeological evidence: it simply corresponds to the location of the various excavations that have taken place at the site. Moreover, like a doubly exposed film, many villages overlap, become partially covered and juxtaposed; one unit was occupied while another was abandoned, but today it appears as though they had been contemporary.

The visitor, therefore, should ignore the present appearance of the countryside and should substitute another image. He should forget the road and the various developments, and extend the slope down to the river, remove the dry-stone terraces and hollow out the ravine that saddles the summit of the hill, so that the rocky spur will be more distinct from the rest of the hillside.

The visitor should also remember that initially only the eastern part of the hill was occupied, that the subsequent villages were cut off from the outside world by a wall, and that it was only later that the village expanded towards the west.

Zone A

Having reached zone A (fig. 40), and facing towards the hill, the visitor will see the remains of the first enclosure wall on the right, which he will be able to follow to the summit of the hill. The original appearance of this wall was altered in places along the 185 m that have been uncovered, after the settlement spread beyond its boundaries by additions which are difficult to interpret. For example, in zone A near unit IA, or in zone C, to the height of building XXV, deep niches have been hollowed out in the wall.

The most impressive unit the visitor will see in zone A is *unit IA*, one of the largest (its external diameter is more than 8 m) and best preserved structures to be excavated at Khirokitia (fig. 41). Its impressive appearance is reinforced by two enormous stone piers, the upper part of which is notched. These were 1.30 m apart and may have supported a platform. The immediate surroundings of the unit – inside which five floor levels have been identified– were altered during its use: to the north, the construction of a retaining wall created a space, a kind of corridor, equipped with domestic installations; to

the south, an annex was added, *unit XIIA*.

Leaving the platform, the steps follow the steep incline of the hill, along the western limit of zone A.

First the visitor sees the remains of *unit XII*, only half of which has been excavated. Mudbricks —coarse rectangles of ochre colour outlined by bonding which appears grey– forming the interior ring of the unit's wall are clearly visible in the trench to the right and left. Elsewhere, on

Fig. 41. Unit IA, 1936 campaign

the other hand, the bricks are of a whitish colour and the bonding is the colour of ochre.

The next structure, *unit V*, is remarkable for the duration of its occupation, which can be subdivided into three phases. The first phase corresponds to floors IX and VIII; it was abruptly interrupted by the collapse of part of the wall. Its reconstruction marks the beginning of the second phase, floors VII to II, during which three adults and five children were buried in the building. There were no significant modifications until the third phase, when an internal circle of stones was added to the structure, thereby reducing the habitable surface area, floor I.

The visitor will pass the ruins of three buildings before reaching *unit XV: XIII* and *XIV* in the foreground, which have not been excavated, and behind them unit X.

It would be more precise to talk of *units X* rather than of unit X, as here there are four superimposed structures. The oldest, X(IV), has an internal diameter of 3 m. The next building phase, X(III), is larger and juts out partially in comparison with the previous one. On one of the floors (X) there is an internal structure of a type found frequently at Khirokitia: a trapezoidal platform, closed on one side by a low dividing wall, and extended by a second, lower platform, supporting a hearth. The plan of the third building phase, X(II), is almost exactly as that of X(IV). There are two steps down from the raised threshold into the house. One of the floors has a

different internal arrangement to that described above: the trapezoidal platform is delimited by two partition walls. Lastly, unit X(I), which is slightly off centre in comparison with the previous phase, has been badly eroded, especially on the south side.

Unit XV also comprises three building phases. Of the oldest, XV(III), only part has been cleared, nothing of which is visible today. The overlying structure, XV(II), is the best preserved. Its wall, comprising a ring of stones on the exterior and a ring of pisé on the interior, has an average thickness of 1.20-1.30 m, which appears disproportionate to the small size of the unit, whose internal diameter measures around 2 m. However, two serious alterations, no doubt caused by the collapse of the upper part of the building, could have increased its internal diameter each time, as in both cases the new wall was set back in comparison to the previous wall. Throughout the occupation of XV(II), which remained in use for some time, seven adults, a child aged five, and ten newborn infants, were buried inside it. The final building phase, XV(I), has been badly damaged by modern terracing.

Built after XV(II), *unit IV* had only a single floor, in the centre of which there was a hearth.

Very close to the first village wall is *unit III*, which underwent several alterations, allowing us to identify four phases of occupation. During the earliest phases, floors X to VI, the internal diameter was around 2.20 m, the entrance was in the southeast, and there were two stairways of four or five steps – one inside, built within the actual wall, and the other outside, up to the threshold. An opening in the wall, 0.45 m high and 0.41 m wide, may have have served as a window. Two niches were also set in the wall. The bodies of a young woman, a middle-aged man, and a newborn baby were found inside this dwelling. Towards the end of this phase, no doubt to consolidate the wall, a supplementary ring of stone and pisé was added to the interior, considerably reducing the habitation area, floors V and IV, and blocking the door, so a new door was added, probably in the east. The third phase, floors III to I, is marked by the construction of a new wall, which did not follow the inside line of the earlier wall. Three burials, two adults and a newborn baby, belong to this phase. The fourth and final phase is represented by the addition of a new internal ring of stones.

The wooden walkway crosses over the enclosure wall of the first village, which is particularly narrow at this point, and continues to a platform, from where there is a view of the whole of zone A, especially the east part of this zone, whilst in the background there is a view of the replica of the neolithic village.

In the foreground we see the remains of two units, wedged one in the other: *unit VIII(II)*, the oldest and smallest, and *unit VIII(I)*.

Beyond this structure is *unit VII*. Only the latest of the three floors was equipped with two rectangular piers, apparently confirming that the piers were not intended to support the roof. Unit VII lies partly over an older structure, *I*, the remains of which can still be seen.

The other units which are visible have only been either marked out *(VI and IX)* or incompletely excavated *(III)*.

Zone B

After climbing further up the hill, the visitor proceeds along zone B (fig. 42), and will see *unit XX* first.

This unit has a roughly circular plan and, like IA, is equipped with two stone piers, which probably supported a platform. The location of the door was modified on several occasions, but only a single floor was identified, covering the burial of four adults. Domestic equipment –two querns installed on a semicircular platform, which is now difficult to see– is found outside the unit, to the south. The two small, unexcavated units to the southeast appear to belong to the same complex as unit XX.

Initially built directly on virgin ground – areas of which, still visible today, allow us to imagine the primitive configuration of this place– the neighbouring unit, *XIX*, was destroyed and immediately rebuilt, at the same time as unit XX. Four floors have been identified in this unit, underneath which seven adult burials were

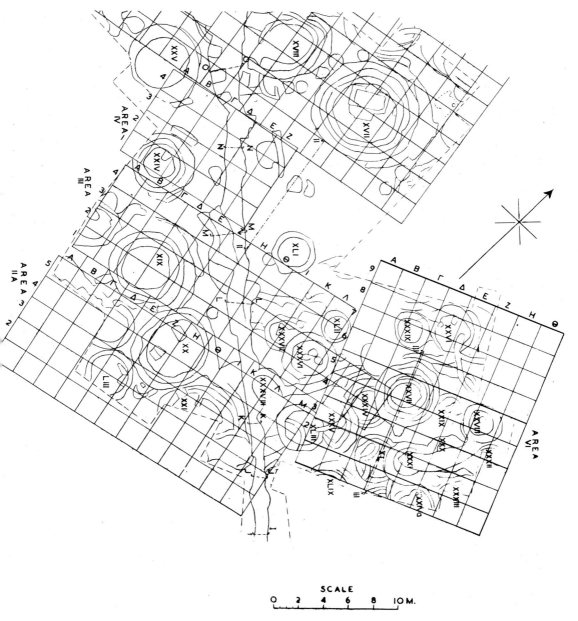

SCALE

0   2   4   6   8   10 M.

Fig. 42.   Plan of zone B

recovered. One of these, a middle-aged woman wearing a cornelian and shell necklace (fig. 43), was placed on fragments of two stone vases that had been broken intentionally. In another burial, an adult, probably a young woman, was lying on her right side, her head resting on five bone tools.

The only noteworthy feature in *unit XXIV* was a triangular pier, whose use is not clear. This was 1 m high and on one side leant against the wall of unit XXIV.

From the stairway it is difficult for the visitor to disentangle the confused remains of the units further east, on the other side of the enclosure wall, especially those of three units –XXVII, XXVIII and XXIX– which open onto an uncovered area, itself closed by a wall and forming a coherent unit. Each of the constituent elements of this house appears to have had a precise function.

The main unit, which was reserved as a living area, appears to have been *unit*

Fig. 43. Burial in unit XIX, 1938 campaign

XXVII, inside which an adult had been buried. Two partition walls divide the dwelling area into two zones, used for distinct activities.

Food must have been cooked in the second unit, *XXVIII*, the centre of which is occupied by a hearth.

These two buildings are linked to each other by a wall enclosing a semicircular space, *unit XXIX*, which is largely open onto the courtyard. This area was reserved for grinding grain and inside there was a quern placed on a platform, 0.5 m high (fig. 44). The flour was collected in a stone tray, found at the foot of the platform. A circular paved area completed this installation.

Zone C

There is little to say about *unit XXV*, the first one which the visitor sees on entering zone C (fig. 45). What appear to be

Fig. 44.   Installation for grinding grain inside unit XXIX, 1939 campaign

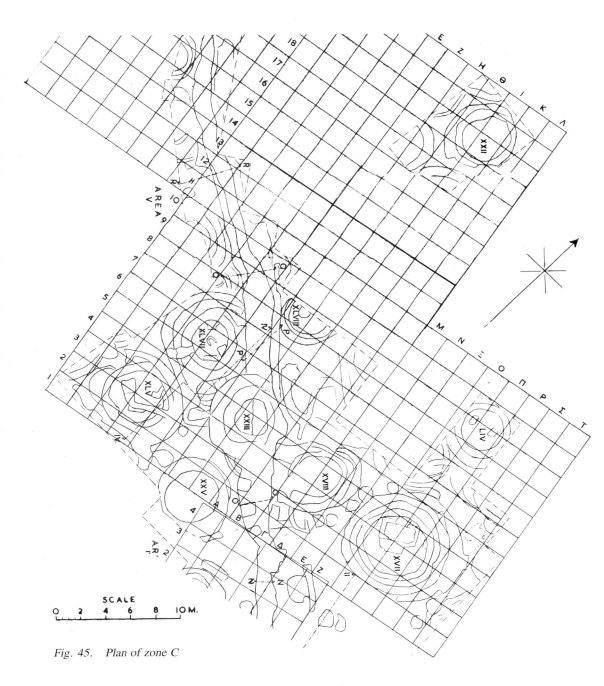

Fig. 45.   Plan of zone C

niches or openings in the wall are in fact a modern alteration: in order to protect the internal ring of mudbrick, the Department of Antiquities had a stone facing built up against the inner face of the wall, but leaving gaps through which the face of the original wall can be seen.

An extension with three niches, of unknown function, was built against the west face of the first village wall level with unit XXV, like that in zone A level with unit IA.

Beyond this wall the visitor can make out the remains of two units: XVII and XVIII.

Unit XVII, with an external diameter of 10 m and an internal diameter of 5 m, is one of the largest units to be excavated at Khirokitia (fig. 46). Although approximately the same size as unit IA, it does not have internal piers. Instead, at some point during its occupation it was equipped with a rectangular platform, 3.20 x 1.60 m, bearing protruding edges on its three sides. A second, smaller platform, 1.60 x

Fig. 46.   Unit XVII, 1938 campaign

1.00 m, was attached to this. Two of the three burials found in the building are notable because of the grave goods which accompanied the deceased. In one, the burial of an adult wearing a necklace of twenty-one cornelian beads alternating with shells, the fragments of three stone vases –that had been broken deliberately– lined the bottom of the grave. The other burial, of an eight-year-old child, contained the beautiful diabase basin shown in figure 32.

Unit XVIII is situated between unit XVII and the village wall. Neither of the unit's two floors yielded any equipment. A young girl was buried inside the unit. Around her neck she wore a necklace of shells, cornelian beads and picrolite, and two stone vases were placed behind her head, one complete and the other broken into several fragments (fig. 47).

Continuing up the hill, the visitor arrives in front of *unit XLV*, with a 2.10 m thick wall of three concentric stone circles. The unit's two piers are arranged differently to those in other houses: one of them leans against the inner face of the wall. Each of the seven burials found inside this unit were of adults; one of them, a man, held a batch of ten bone tools in his right hand.

The adjacent unit, *XLVII*, is the one most often cited to demonstrate that these units were domed. Based on the inward curvature of a section of this unit's wall, P. Dikaios put forward a reconstruction of a stone and pisé dome, which he estimated to be 3.70 m in height, the internal diameter of the building being 3 m. Undoubtedly, a portion of the wall is clearly sloping, but there is nothing to suggest that this is part of a dome rather than a section of the wall which has leant over. The procedure most commonly used to achieve a vault is corbelling, with the individual, horizontally superimposed elements overlapping each other without exerting lateral push, yet nothing of the sort is apparent here. Instead the wall in its entirety appears to have toppled over. Moreover, to the north the visitor can see a mudbrick wall, the layers of which are not horizontal, as might be expected, but instead lean to the south – that is to say with the same incline as the so-called superstructure. Now, it should not be forgotten that Khirokitia is built on the side of a hill, and that the slope is often steep, as can be seen inside unit XIX. Therefore the pressure of the earth is significant and could well be the cause of the distortion of the walls, particularly noticeable on their upper part, where the pressure exerted by the soil is the strongest. On the other hand, the lower part of the wall, when it is not damaged by erosion, more often juts out. Also, impressive though the curvature towards the interior of part of the wall of unit XLVII may be, it does not justify the reconstruction of a domed roof.

Occupied over a long period –eight occupation levels have been identified– unit XLVII had been altered on several occasions, and its present appearance is deceptive. The wall of stone and mud-brick lies on a stone substructure, and was opened in the southwest by a door, with gypsum slabs covering the jambs and threshold. The doorway was reached by steps both inside and out.

As well as for its architectural elements this building is notable for the number and nature of its burials: twenty-four out of a total of twenty-nine burials were those of newborn babies.

Unit XXIII, which is partly built on the first village enclosure wall, illustrates the moment when the village spread beyond its initial confines towards the west. This extension into previously unoccupied land was accompanied by the construction of a new enclosure wall, the remains of which are visible in zone D.

Zone D

The most important remains to have come to light in this zone (figs 3 and 48), which

Fig. 47.   Burial in unit XVIII, 1938 campaign

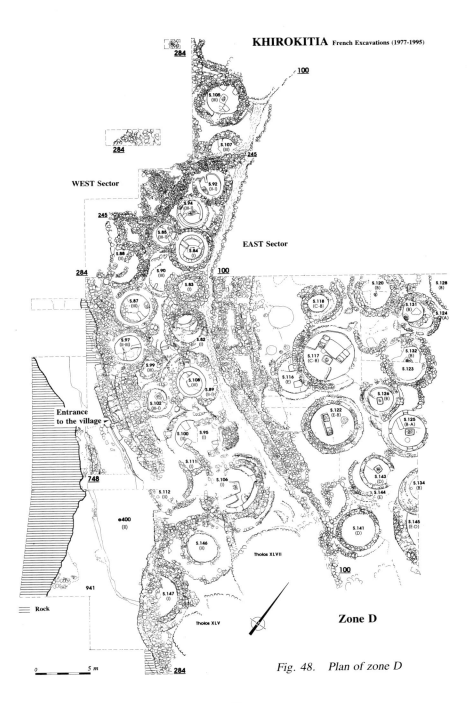

KHIROKITIA French Excavations (1977-1995)

WEST Sector

EAST Sector

Entrance to the village

≡ Rock

Fig. 48.   Plan of zone D

Zone D

0   5 m

is still being excavated, are not the remains of the wall, impressive though it is, but rather the remains of one of the entrances, or to be more precise, one of the entrance systems into the village. The visitor has already seen its replica at the foot of the site. This construction is peculiar to Cyprus and the Near East and demonstrates the exceptional technical expertise of the inhabitants of Khirokitia (fig. 49). It is a complex system, the various elements of which the visitor can see in the foreground, and responds to two different needs: it compensates for the difference in height of more than 2 m between the surface on which the village was built and that outside the wall, without creating on opening in the wall, and it controls access to the village. The main element, added onto the external face of the village enclosure wall, is a large stone structure with carefully plastered faces.

Fig. 49.   One of the entrances to the neolithic village

Fig. 50.   View of zone D, east sector, during excavation. In the foreground, unit S. 125; in the background, S. 122 in the centre, and S. 117 to the right

Within this structure there was a stairway which turned in three flights at right angles. Entry from the outside was controlled by a second architectural element: a stone structure that appears to lean against a rock projection.

Having cleared this first hurdle, a person entering the village would then have to climb the first flight of steps, then turn left, to climb the second flight, and finally turn once again to the right, to mount the third flight. He would then find himself on top of the entrance wall, which, after again turning right, he would have to follow for several metres before finally arriving inside the village, no doubt descending steps which have yet to be excavated.

Fig. 51.   Unit S. 117

In the background the remains of the first village stretch between the summit of the hill, which has been stripped by erosion so that no architectural remains survive, and the wall that the visitor has been able to follow from zone A (fig. 50).

Among the most remarkable units in this zone is *unit S. 122* (fig. 15). This unit was erected shortly after the foundation of the settlement, and was inhabited without interruption over a long period. The interior surface of its wall and the faces of the notched pillars standing more or less in the centre of the building have painted decoration (fig. 13). The burial of an individual accompanied by the ritual already described was found inside this unit.

Unit S. 117, which adjoins S. 122, also has two notched piers, which were joined by a platform at some point during its occupation (fig. 51).

Unit *S. 125*, close to S. 122 with which it was functionally linked for a time, also deserves to be pointed out. It is, in effect, one of the rare examples of a unit which has windows (figs 10 and 50) at regular intervals. These two units, S. 117 and S. 125, have been reconstructed identically at the foot of the site.

THE VISITORS' CENTRE AND THE ARCHAEOLOGICAL PARK

The very great increase in the number of tourists in the ten years between 1980-1990, and also their negative effect upon the ancient monuments and archaeological sites poses a pressing problem for the protection of the antiquities of Cyprus.

The visitors, welcome though they are, inevitably contribute to the accelerated deterioration of the sites and of the natural environment. Therefore, to protect the archaeological heritage of the island and, at the same time, to improve the services offered to visitors, the Ancient Monuments section of the Department of Antiquities of Cyprus has initiated a comprehensive series of projects. Foreign specialists are supervising the study of the projects for the sites of Paphos, Kourion and Kouklia; whereas the service of Ancient Monuments itself was in charge of the study and completion of the project for the site of Khirokitia.

The philosophy of the project is to preserve the authenticity of the neolithic site in its entirety, to protect the human and natural surroundings, and to provide richer information by the creation of a Visitors' Centre. The Visitors' Centre acts as an intermediary between the archaeological remains and the modern visitor, who sometimes has problems interpreting them.

In the case of Khirokitia, instead of constructing a modern building, it was thought preferable to reconstruct five neolithic units, part of the enclosure wall and one of the entrances to the site, identical copies of the original structures. The French Mission currently excavating the site provided all the information concerning the construction materials, the plans, and the dimensions of the buildings.

The units were built, using traditional techniques, of mudbrick, pisé and other materials. All the construction materials are from around the site and from the bed of the Maroni River which runs alongside the village.

The replica, in its entirety, is at the moment one of the few examples of this genre in Cyprus. Various problems arose during the construction of the units, which were discussed by architects, masons and archaeologists. The solutions chosen were always those which appeared most likely to have been used by prehistoric man.

The solutions adopted for the roofs were taken from archaeological discoveries, principally the imprints on fragments of earth from a collapsed roof, which provided precious information as to the materials used and the shape of the roof.

Inside the houses there are both authentic neolithic artefacts and copies, illustrating daily life. Agriculture provided the main dietary requirements, and this is reflected by the plants growing in the neighbourhood of the reconstruction, which are those which had been cultivated during the Neolithic.

The funerary practices are also presented inside the units, as are the domestic installations, such as hearths and platforms used as work and rest areas.

One unit was left incomplete to show the different stages of construction and the materials employed.

Before climbing the hill, the visitor will find relevant publications in several languages, in the Visitors' Centre, which is like an archaeological park. These give information about the side and will prepare the visitor for his visit to the archaeological remains.

Various information points around the site help the visitors orientate themselves, and complement the guide. There are two terraces with a panorama over the site which, on a clear day, give a general view of the neolithic village.

SOPHOCLES HADJISAVVAS

BIBLIOGRAPHY

DIKAIOS P., *Khirokitia*. Final Report on the Excavation of a Neolithic Settlement in Cyprus on behalf of the Department of Antiquities 1936-1946. Monograph of the Department of Antiquities of the Government of Cyprus no. 1. Oxford: Oxford University Press, 1953.

GJERSTAD E., *Finds and Results of the Excavations in Cyprus, 1927-1931. The Swedish Cyprus Expedition* I. Stockholm 1934.

LE BRUN A., *Un site néolithique précéramique en Chypre: Cap Andreas-Kastros, Paris: A.D.P.F., 1981.*

— *Fouilles récentes à Khirokitia (Chypre), 1977-1981.* Paris: Editions Recherche sur les Civilisations, 1984.

— *Fouilles récentes à Khirokitia (Chypre), 1983-1986.* Paris: Editions Recherche sur les Civilisations, 1989.

— *Fouilles récentes à Khirokitia (Chypre), 1988-1991.* Paris: Editions Recherche sur les Civilisations, 1994.

TODD I. A., *Vasilikos Valley Project 6: Excavations at Kalavasos-Tenta,* I. Studies in Mediterranean Archaeology, vol. LXXIX: 6. Göteborg: Paul Åströms Förlag, 1987.

THE ENGLISH EDITION
OF KHIROKITIA, A NEOLITHIC SITE
WRITTEN BY ALAIN LE BRUN
AND TRANSLATED BY LOUISE STEEL
WAS PUBLISHED IN 5000 COPIES
IN FEBRUARY 1997
FOR THE BANK OF CYPRUS
CULTURAL FOUNDATION.
THE BOOK WAS PREPARED BY M.L. MITSOU
AND PRINTED BY CHR. NICOLAOU & SON.
EDITOR OF THE GUIDE BOOKS SERIES
IS MARIA IACOVOU